Table of contents

Entrepreneurship imagination

Published by Liberty Chidziwa at Createspace

Preface

This book is a nugget of wisdom to the entrepreneurs who wish to be in business and those already operating in various business ventures. It offers research based solutions with a practical "out of the box" information. Imagination or creativity is what everybody wants besides the theories and models in management or business books. What is left unanswered in these books is the practical part of the "in the field" and experience for creativity which is the best teacher. This book answers that gap and attempts to explain the day to day mind programming activities that lead to the realisation of dreams.Enjoy it!

ENTREPRENUERSHIP IMAGINATION

Published by Liberty Chidziwa at Createspace

CHAPTER 1: IMAGINATION MAGIC

"Success is forged in the furnace of inspiration and yearnings passions of achievement."Vincent Pearl

Brain power

The capacity of the human mind in creativity is far reaching. We dream, imagine and create things through the brainpower. The faculties given to us is a God given tool beyond measure. One business expert quoted that, "The brains are the biggest capital a person can have, which is equivalent to a valuable asset if not more than the asset. It is precious asset that one possesses, not only financial capital as people often think. It is part of the intellectual capital and that is why some people are paid for their ideas. In imagination magic; there is a big room for success in any business venture that you may think of. You must know that the brain is like a gem of diamond hidden, a nugget just inside us and if we unleash it to its potential, great exploits will happen that we never thought of. Most of us are crying foul in life citing that we are poor, when we actually have everything very powerful inside us.

Success in Business -A Condition of the mind

Success in life is a continuum. At one end, there is failure and at the other opposite there is satisfaction. Success begins with failure to most people in life or business and usually ends up with great acomplishment.You have to acknowledge that failure is part of the ingredients of success and life is blended with different ingredients in each step of the way. Take each step at a time in building a successful legacy called **SUCCESS PILLAR**. Emerson wrote, "Successfulness in business depends on a plus condition of your mind and body or the power of work and courage. Conditioning of the mind is a great battle of many people because of doubt, fear and past bad history. In life the mind need to be conditioned or programmed for success. The same conditioning is needed to a business entity.

Enthusiasm and brain power

Enthusiasm generates immense power in your plans. Most business plans of organisations lack this charisma especially when you read them and even the funders fail to feel this enthuasism.Ambition and energy are the key elements to make things happen in what you will do in business, but it must start inside your cranium-the brain. The brain has eyes and grasps reality of things .It magnifies your vision and visualises things happening before they exist and it has a clear picture. This is the quality with us human beings which makes us unique as compared with the animal kingdom. We see things in the abstract before they happen and draw them near our view like a pair binoculars lens do.

Zelig Plikskin has proved right by his most interesting powerful exercise for many people. He says," Imagine a great source of power surrounding you. Visualise this energy permeating and penetrating your whole being .Close your eyes as if you fill every cell and every neuron recharging with new energy. Breathe deeply, as the energy source of inspiration is charging you". This is a stimulating exercise before you can do something challenging. Inspired brains can change the world, change business entities and even change ourselves.

Self programming for success

You will get what you create with your thoughts. Get this clear in mind that attainment of goals in a business is a product of what was programmed in the subconscious mind of the owners or the managers. It could have been moulded in the strategic planning meetings or created individually as one was meditating alone. For business plans and strategic planning to be achieved, firstly there is need for crafting these concepts or maxims in the brains. You need to unleash your power by setting goals that are exiting enough to inspire your creativity and ignite passion. Because passion is magnetic, where it is living, there is power. Goals are tangible things to propel you into action. Speak them, pray over them, brood over them and they will manifest. If the brain is coded with positive information, it will see and catapult you to greater heights and dimensions. There is nothing like abstract in the brain because it is us who cannot see it, not with the brains .As long you can dream, you can create anything. As long as you are alive, you must hope for the best. Self programme your mind with greatest words from different role models and mentors. the secrets of successful business people and you will see amazing patterns of their words

Dreams come true

Many people do believe that dreams come true. Believe me, you are focussed they will come true. Remember, it is important to have great personal plans, business plans and strategic plans put on paper. Do not just dream and let those dreams evaporate without taking time to put them on paper to materialise them. Once there are on paper, it's easy to feel them and be in contact with them. That is the reason why a business plan is so important and that is why companies display mission statements on the walls.

Never lose focus, but keep on in the track and throw your dreams on board into action and you will see them coming to superb reality. Time for the materiality of the dream does not matter. Time belongs to God. Tom Clancy said, "Nothing is as real as a dream. The world can change around you, but your dreams do not. Responsibilities need to erase them, but they cannot change those dreams. Duties need to obscure it, but because the dream is within you, no one can take it away or possess it. It is within your view alone and the achievement of them is just between you and your dream. Infact, there is no distance between your dream and you. It is your heritage, a legacy and it will manifest at the appointed time.Habbakuk the prophet of God was even told to write the vision, and make it plain upon tables for everyone to read. This is a golden secret.

James Allen, the greatest motivational speaker said, "He who cherishes a beautiful vision, a lofty one in his heart, he/she will realise it someday. You must dream big dreams, and so shall you become .This is true to one verse in the Bible which says, "For as he thinketh in his heart, so is he "(Proverbs 23v7).Remember there is no medicine or antidote in life like having hope. No incentive so great and no tonic as powerful as expectation of something tomorrow. It heals your spirit. Keep on hoping on your dream

Chapter 2 .Walk your dream

"Happiness is an attitude of the mind born of simple determination to be happy under outward circumstances" J.Donald Walters

Feeling your dream

As you dream for a big business, it is important to feel your dream. Jean Tommer has the greatest principles of faith when he says,"Talk about it only enough to do it, dream enough only to feel it and think enough to understand it. Finally, contemplate it only enough to be in it'"

What Jean Tommer meant here is a cornerstone of dreaming principles. It means we must talk, but it is important to make action. Propel your words into action .Do not just talk like a talk show, walk the talk. It reminds of Charles Blondin, the great tight rope walker who asked people whether they believed he could cross the Niagara Falls with someone in the wheelbarrow. Everybody replied with a big YES. When he asked from the crowd for a volunteer in the wheelbarrow, nobody dared to risk his life. Imagine how many people want to open or start a business? They are plenty plus! The reason they are not in business is that they are afraid to lose their money. They do not want to come from the comfort zone.

For dreams to be achieved, they must be felt in action. Feel it and let it be part of you for there is nothing that can hinder you .No demon from hell can steal your dream .The secret is you and inside you.

The art of imagination

The greatest end is to strike the imagination chord. With the power of the soul that refuses not to admit defeat even in the middle of a collapsing world, keep going tough. Greatest artists do not have a true picture of what they want to paint. They just paint from imagination and see a brighter side, add a brighter colour and they come up with a unique bright picture. You will not believe it! Many of us will never cease to wonder how the artists have painted such a masterpiece picture. It is the from the ability to see the unseen and make it real. Take a pen, write your dreams and make it a policy to read them as often as you can.

Create your opportunity

It is you who create opportunity through innovative ideas. Most people who invented new things, for example Thomas Edison who invented the light bulb, created his opportunity which is a legacy to him and his family until now. It is so with most gifted entrepreneurs, who created opportunities for themselves. They did not wait for Mr Opportunity to knock at their doors, but they created it on their own. They saw needs hidden in the market before others realised them and made a great leap into the opportunity doors to make billions of money. When others who were snoring woke up, Mr Opportunity wings were brightening as his flew away faster.Gone! Yes, he cannot wait for the snoring.

The realised Mr Opportunity disappeared in thin air! Therefore, it means you can create opportunity by yourself and turn crises into creative opportunities, defeats into success and frustration into fullfilment.How is it possible? Use your great self asset, your self esteem which is the 'invisible weapon' around you. Stand up and stand tall and stamp your creative impression on everything and make it the agent of your will and the executor of your purpose.Remember,opportunities avail themselves to those who have living dreams that are sound and it is attracted to the true dreamers who are prepared.

Imagination is risky

Of course the outcome in life or business is not always so triumphant. Remember the Apple Newton (1993-1998)? This tablet failed because of the shoddy battery life and hard-to-read screen. Apple Corporation had also ten old products that failed in the market and did not hit the intended mark. This was considered a colossal failure at the time. It turns out it was simply a great idea ahead of its time. Herein lays the problem with using your imagination. You run the risk of coming up with something people just are not ready for. Humiliation and ridicule is quite common, which is why so many choose imitation over imagination. It feels safer. But no one ever changed the world by playing it safe.

For example, I am working on something right now that takes a radically different approach to delivering content to book lovers. Will it be a hit? Perhaps. Will it be a flop? Well, if I go purely by statistics and what is currently on the market, one must conclude the odds are not in my favor. Then again, had Apple gone by statistics and the market at the time, we would have no iPhone or iPad. Some will argue that Apple had a strong position with the iPod that made the iPhone possible. True, but what about the iPod? At the time, it was just another MP3 player. Now it is the best tablet producer from a 20 years experimental failure that is from 1993 to 2013.

Creative problem solving requires creative thinking which requires imagination--lots of it. Look at your business and dig deep into the inner regions of your imagination. What can you do that is radically different than everyone else? Not different for difference sake, but something that can have a real and positive impact for your customers or your industry. The best part is that you don't have to invent something new. Just make some important tweaks and put yourself out there. Maybe you will flop. So what? It may just be your own Newton experience--a major failure that paves the way to your big breakthrough.

Chapter 3: Business planning

"You do things when the opportunities come along .I have had periods in my life when I had a bundle of ideas come along and I have had long dry spells. If I get an idea next week I will do something. If not, I won't do damn things." Warren Buffett

This topic is delving deep into the deep aspects which any aspiring entrepreneur will want to know about planning. Most people who want to go into a business know that business needs- a tangible business plan with concrete ideas .Banks, financiers and funders need to see it in black and white as well. Warren Buffet, a prominent World Billionaire ranking at number one in 2014, advocates that you only have to do a very few things right in your life so long you do not do too many things wrong. To minimise these errors in life a business plan is needed

Business plan

It is a written plan expressed into monetary value. In general, a business plan is simple to write and craft (check my other detailed business plans on Smashwords). The first thing is to do is to discover your key competences you are talented in. Never delve into a business which you do not have knowledge about. Too many people have lost money or wealth because of entering into an idea that was suggested by a friend, internet or other people have suggested .Take time in planning, but be quick to make a decision. Always follow your plans which you have taken time to create

Components of a business plan
The business plan should have

- Introduction or executive summary
- Management segment
- Marketing segment
- Human resources segment

- Strategy and implementation segment
- Financial segment
- Appendix

These are the basic expected topics to be seen in the business plan subtopics.

Critical aspects about a business plan

Before you think of having a business plan, the best advice I suggest is to check the ones on Smashwords eBooks. They are cheaper and can help you to generate your own idea. An average business plan which is about 15-25 pages can cost more than US$100 from business planners unlike the US$10-US$19 price range which you can get from the internet .You can modify it to make yours. Brilliant! If you decide to approach business plan consultants, make sure you approach them with your vision in mind .The vision belongs to you and the consultant must not erase or write another vision which is different from yours. Most people who used to come to our consultancy office for business plans without an idea .They ended up convinced into ideas which were not compatible to their original plan. Do not just take anything because you do not have an idea for business. This was so because clients came without a clear specific vision and we would suggest the next best alternative. The problem is that as consultants we may suggest an idea, but it's up to you to stick to your vision. Never falter in your dream for the second best dream. Maybe it is not your calling or it's not your revealed area by God and this may cause a failure at the end. Again, never get forced into a business venture opposite to your vision because there is a high chance of failure. The reason is simple; it is not part of you.

The other practical thing about a business plan is that it must be well organised, short and precise. The idea must be clear and well spelt and as I alluded before. It must be your idea .The financial segment is the most important area and it must be done by an expert who is good in financial accounting. It must be correctly calculated though these are projections of the future business. Additionally, it must have analysis of ratios and the financial health of the business (cash flow), because financial institutions need to assess almost two things profitability and liquidity. They need to see whether your business is viable or not and it must have less risk .It must generate sales more than operational costs. On the liquidity side, it must be able to pay back the money borrowed back as soon as possible or over a certain period. Some banks need a payment schedule calculated of the borrowed principal (initial amount) with the interest accrued .This is just a projection of the money to be paid back. This is usually shown at the appendix segment.

The other important aspect before you write your own business plan for a bank is that, first go and see a bank consultant and ask their requirements needed for approval of loans. If it is possible bring a draft document for correction to the bank. Then it will be easy because all critical areas would have been polished by the bank consultant. Another method that is useful is to ask an expert business plan consultant to visit your bank on your behalf and see your bank consultant. The language of accounting, finance or business jargon may not be familiar with many people so it's easier to leave the burden to your consultant, but remember not to lose your vision you dreamed.Becareful to leave your plans everywhere when you are writing them, because your ideas may be stolen. Duplication of ideas is easily detected by the banks and usually the one who will steal it may come first at the bank before you come with your plan for submission. Obviously, you cannot convince the bank that the idea is yours. Believe me; ideas are stolen that is why when you give a business idea to the business plan consultant, making sure you sign a confidentiality agreement. Your idea is worth billions of dollars before it is implemented.

Time management and planning

So often we experience time as fleeting, frenetic and pressured. It is important we have effective time management skills in our changing world. Bill Gates noted something about our ideas. He said", Intellectual property has the shelf life of a banana. "The key issue is that when you have a brilliant ideas do not delay to implement it or wait for time because it will expire. Yes expiring, being outdated in other words.

Once you put it in black and white, then try to implement it before someone, somewhere else duplicates your idea as a new entrant in the market you are targeting. Harvard

Business Professor, Michael Porter, warned of the new entrants in the business as part of the five threats in the micro environment. New entrants are unavoidable and some of them maybe very powerful than you or they can duplicate your idea and modify it. For example, in the technological industry, Apple duplicated the idea of IBM in 1980, five years later when IBM had already started, but now it is leading in the tablet market though it had failure in the PC market.

Personal strategic plan

The majority of us operate like wildlife animals if I may be allowed to be frank enough. Why? Sometimes we live like wanderers not having a purpose or not having specific goals in life. The majority of people are focused on base goals of food, shelter, clothing and sex.Maslow identified them as the lowest needs which are nearest if not equal to the "goals" of the wildlife kingdom. A human being is supernatural more than wildlife animals because we can see the future and have the ability to plan. Human beings have an instinct for the need of achievement and personal drive ego which is underutilised by us.A personal strategic plan is a guideline of personal long-term goals put in black and white usually done at the beginning of the year. However, personal planning goes back to proper time management. Most of people do not even have one in ink. They may be written in diaries, but maybe soon forgotten for anything that comes away in the course of life. Some do value company strategic plans and even attend long meetings in companies, but do not take a serious step to sit down and come to basics to have self introspection and project the future ahead.Personal strategic plans may be for families, couples and individuals. It must have goals which are specific, timeframed, attainable, measurable and realistic. But, do not stop dreaming big because your potential is greater than you may think. The other thing important is to include areas like, diet, exercise, leisure, personal branding, vision, goals, education, marriage and other topics specific to you. Start it now if you did not have one!

Be organised

The first thing God put in place in the creation of this universe was order and we must be orderly "upstairs". For example, there are things we must plan for the next 2 years, 5 years and 10 years. However, the steps of tomorrow are shaped by today's seconds ticking. The tools such as diaries and wrist watches are often used at workplaces, but not on a personal capacity to self improve one's time management skills.In business time means money and money means time. Did you get it? Time is very crucial and remember that a day that has passed without focussing about your plans is a wasted day.

Take action

The majority of people are in the valley of despair or the in abyss of failure dreaming on the hammock, lying there never to think tomorrow may come again. Some booze to sooth away their worries without taking time to pursue their goals.Action is the result of auto programmed thoughts. It becomes a sin to God and nature to plan and plan without taking action.Idly waiting or procrastination is a time wasting activity and an opportunity stealer. Remember, life is a journey of inspiration and motivation.Nothing is achieved without your zeal and enthuasism.The technological world we are in is also having its delusions to the youths who think life it's just at the click of the mouse to make things happen.The principles of hard work are ignored, but they still stands unchanged. No pain no gain, no gain no pain. Take action and be bold to forget your failures and take action according to your strategic plan

The principles of life are tried and tested by those who have trod the way of life especially the aged ones who are experienced with it. Betting for a lottery, sudden riches and where one gains wealth by the hook and crook method should not be followed .These are dead end roads to success-you never reach anywhere, but end up in the abyss of defeat and remorse. Even the words of the bible from the wisest man Solomon, suggest that,"'Whatever your hand find to do, do it with all thy might. "Refuse to eat the bread of idleness and refuse to receive gifts always, but instead learn to give gifts to others.

Chapter 4: Greatest Imaginators

It is better to hang out with people better than you. Pick associates whose behaviour is better than yours and you will drift in that direction .Warren Buffet

Benchmark with the excellent

Napoleon Hill discovered that thoughts are tangible things and if mixed with definiteness of purpose, persitance and a burning desire for their translation into riches and other material objects, they will materialise.

In business, benchmark with the best or the champions of the industry.Benchmark your service with the best not against the mediocre service providers. Iron sharpens iron, so is the best sharpens the upcoming best.Role modelling is very important in entreprenuership.Everything in the company should convey a badge of excellence and that is Total Quality Management principles. Excellence start with the owner and it can be seen in everything as a corporate culture.

Innovative Imaginators

In 2014 July ,Mark Zugerberg at 23 years age was worth 30 billion US dollars.It is none other than the Facebook social network, the most popular social network.Facebook is having almost a billion subscribers.Zugerberg started his novel idea with Harvard students by creating a social network of old Harvard University former students. The idea came from his computer programming skills at a very tender age. The experiment with Harvard old students struck a creative idea in his mind that caused him to launch it in 2004.Luck was on his side, the idea worked excellently.

Bill Gates, a Harvard university dropout started Micro-Soft by then in 1975.He had a passion in computer programming and he invented the computer package solutions of the Microsoft .He is the best well-known computer business entrepreneur if not a brand name in the computer world. What is spectacular about him is that, at the university, he spent more time on the computer than study. In 1975, he saw an opportunity of a software which was demand   related to the Intel 8080 CPU, the one he was good at in software engineering .He was bold to talk his decision to his parents who supported the idea of forming a company .He was also joined by a college Paul Allen who had a shared vision like his and both formed a company called Microsoft. It is funny to note that he never came back to finish his degree at Harvard University. In other words, he defied odds and popular belief that education can make you successful in life.

Henry Ford saw an ox drawn wagon and spoke of the engine drawn wagon replacing the horse drawn wagons. He is credited for his never dying persistence and innovative ideas. Ford Motors, in 2008 was nearly 188billion, a fortune made by one imaginative entrepreneur.

Christopher Columbus, the great Italian admiral, had a passion for the sea at a young boy. He dreamed of undiscovered worlds and had a passion for conquering them. Columbus had an adventurous spirit. In his biography, he earns three titles which are very spectacular, one of an explorer; the second of a navigator and the third of a coloniser. He discovered Hispaniola and is credited for the discovery of America too. Before he took his long journeys Columbus consulted from astrologers, merchants, sea captains and geographers. He amassed a lot of information and it is reported that he could tell the directions accurately by the stars with explicit accuracy. He was such a determined individual.

Thomas Edison off course is the well known for failing 10,000 times in the trying to make a bulb. His persistence is unbelievable in that he could continue with the experiments with such numerous disappointments. Maybe he was crazy or he had some crazy passions, some people can say that. He finally managed to make the electric bulb and when he was asked why he made so many attempts he replied."I was learning 10,000 times of not making a bulb". Such a blunt but challenging answer showed that he never believed in giving up.

The Wright brothers dreamed and wished one day to be like birds.It took a number of years for their project and they became the first to become the pioneers of the aeroplane. Another great entrepreneur is Neil Armstrong who had a discovering and adventurous spirit. In 1969, after a carefully but risk project, he landed on the moon and put the Union Jack flag as a sign of a mission accomplished.

Greatest Imaginators coming

The world we are living is ushering greatest entrepreneurs who challenge the odds and who have the audacity to create new things breaking new grounds. What is surprising is that these people are just like you and me, but the difference is the persistence and in the way they see opportunities. Their imaginative part of the mind is creative, be it in the business or sporting world. We will see a lot of promising entrepreneurs with novelty, brilliant ideas and amazing ideas. Most of these guys are taking advantage because of technology

Chapter 5.Creative words

"'Failure is simply the opportunity to begin again this time more intelligently.'"
Henry Ford

Spoken words

If you carefully study the life of champions, you will realise that their words have something magnetic with them. They are successful because they spoke of success often. They still speak positively about success and success in inherent in their lives. The charisma and magic of words has greatly helped a lot of people to come from abysses of defeat the victory mountain top. Oliver Wendell Holmes says," A word is not a crystal, transparent and unchanged, it is the skin of a living thought and may vary greatly in colour and content according to circumstances and in time in which it is used". It is true words clothes the inherent thoughts hidden in the subconscious mind.

Remember, that the world which we inhabiting came from the spoken words. God only spoke out the words which had the creative power to shape billion of things which we see and some of them we cannot see. The world is surprisingly hanging in a space at an unchanging angle never falling. Why? It is still obeying the words spoken from the beginning. The sea waves never cross even their demarcated boundaries. Even scientists acknowledge that all matter has sound waves in them. The sound waves are still vibrating in matter until now. Words have an anointing effect. What you dream and what you say will surely happen.

Most wisdom books explain that positive words are essential to stimulate positive results and positive lifestysles.Even the words of the bible agree with wisdom from different religions and theories in psychology on the impact of self affirmation of positive words. Investigate them; you will see one thing that they have a never dying maxim about the creative effect of words. The speaking of great words of inspiration is typical of great champions .Their words are captivating and stimulating. This is the reason why seminars, workshops and motivation workshops are done. Motivational speakers are highly paid for shaping dreams of people and resurrecting dead dreams in tombs of despair.

Never talk defeat or failure

When you write your business plans, personal plans and your life goals, the very good thing is to speak over them. See their picture, see the profits and see the future and the destiny you want and then prophesy it in words. Affirmation of such great words sink in the realm of your spirit and your thoughts .They will create your vision as you put into action your plans. The plans will roll following the words dictated to them.All things in this word listen to the power or authority in you. One famous man of God said,"I will never be defeated"'. He was affirming them in faith and for sure his ministry is a beacon of his words. Never utter defeat of doubt. Change your vocabulary from words like maybe,failure,sickness,loss,broke,and speak positive words like I'm sure,Im certain, am strong, my business is progressing and Iam sufficient with money. Encode your tongue to speak the plans and speak success-it will be yours definitely! Walter Westfall advocated that it takes only a few words to destroy someone's hopes and dreams and it takes a few words to give reason and start to dream again. That is why people buy books about motivational books, attend seminars and workshops. This is the purpose of this book and that is to inspire you to programme your words. The main purpose is to get inspiration of words and then take off. Life needs taking off like an aeroplane which takes off against wind not in the direction with wind. Captains of the seas cut across seas and sail against winds to reach the shore. The same is going to happen to you. Splendid!

Some people think that positive speaking is wishful thinking.No, it is a dream manifestation method; it is the dream shaping and materialisation of reality. The human spirit need to be conditioned for success. Be passionate about your goals and passionate about your destiny by always speaking their achievement.

Destructive words

Most children are encoded with the wrong words when they grow up and even whilst they are still in their womb. Parents have a healing, blessing and cursing effect on the future of their children. They must not utter negative statements on children. It also takes words to revoke any curses of misfortunes inside someone's life. Study on your own, you will realise that spiritualism, occult and witchcraft is hinged on the principle of speaking forth. They understand the importance of words than we do and use them for destruction and accomplish their dreams. The moment people believe what they are told and affirm with their mouths, and then it is sure to happen sometime or in the future. It may be positive or negative, but it will surely happen.

How many people failed exams or interviews because they voiced it out? Or how many people who got sick because they always affirmed that they will be sick oneday? Others got their businesses in liquidity problems because they were caught with fear and believed it. The moment the stock market fell and people spoke badly about investing in their company, they believed it and got stroke or heart attack without even seeing the results. That is why companies need people called public relations managers who will constantly speak positively about the company's image even at times when things are rock bottom spiralling at the company. It is a sure remedy in bringing the business confidence in investors. The best thing you can do to negative words is to be adamant about them. Do not give an ear. Do not listen people who speak small about you and against your dreams.

Chapter 6: Passionate presence

"Nothing limits achievement like small thinking, nothing expands possibilities like unleashed imagination "William Author Ward

Fish story-A great lesson

Catherine Ingram tells a story about a small fish who swims to an older fish and says"', You go on and on in water, I have been searching for it and nowhere to be found .I have studied all the texts ,practised and trained diligently and met with those who have known it ,but it eluded me."'The old fish says, "Yes my son, as Iam saying that not only you are swimming into it right now, but you are part of it and you are composed of it". The young fish shakes his head in frustration and says, "Maybe I will find it someday." We are so like the small fish in our lives .We search everywhere outside ourselves and try to find ourselves.We collect experiences, relationships; knowledge and objects. We hope to get praise to validate our significance. But while we seek, research and quest for reality in pleasures, we forget to find our hidden gift-our own PASSIONATE PRESENCE.

Usually people adventure with the joys of life and look for beauty outside somewhere. What is known as passionate presence is merely feeling the immaculate consciousness here and now, realising the gift in our sphere of influence in us.It is fully present with us. In business, we should realise our sphere of influence and utilise it.Noone can disturb your sphere of influence or take it.

Which business to start dilemma

This is a greatest question with many people. Everybody needs to start a business or a new venture mainly for financial freedom reason. Many books have been written about starting a business, but what is left unanswered is the software needed in the entrepreneurs .But the key question still remains, which business can I start? Some just follow ideas of colleagues, family, teachers or a mentor's advice. It is not bad, but the best advice I would suggest is to start the business which is linked to your passionate presence.In other words what is your hidden talent? What is that you are passionate in?

The greatest entrepreneurs are those who discover their strengths and obtain a college degree or diploma in that area and then pursue their area of interest. Never copy someone's ideas because it may not be your calling. This is the reason why most start ups fail early before they take off. It is because someone told him or her that there are quick bucks in that nature of business.

Again on the other of the continuum, there are some people who have defied tradition beliefs or odds by starting something totally different from their education. I have seen accountants graduate into engineering field for life, computer engineer becoming doctors, tourism people becoming accountants or lawyers becoming CAs. (Chartered Accountants.)The reason is that people failed to discover their PASSIONATE PRESENCE.They later diverted their plans to their true callings unknowingly, some by divine providence, others by chance. On the other side of the coin, we see people who have been career guided while very young to what they must become.They believed it and embraced it that I'm a so and so person or I will do the following course when I grow up. With purposefulness, they succeeded and became what they are now.

Discover your calling

It must be within the individual to be able to feel his or her passionate presence .It can be felt especially when one is growing or some find it by discovery. If you are an IT person then do businesses in IT and if are an accountant then look for businesses in accounting eg consulting or auditing.Many people have left companies to start their own companies. Self employed,I may say so .The majority were employed in certain skills which they converted to use in their own companies. This reduces the risk of failure as you are an expert in that area because knowledge is power.However, most imaginative entrepreneurs,discover new opportunities by experimenting and exploring. They will find new ideas when they are in the field and choose exactly what they are good at.

Positive self image

The passionate presence inside you will tell you that this is my area or my calling.This passionate presence is felt even in the people with whom you meet. Several times when my spirit was highly inspired, people would see the composure and confidence coming out from me.I ended up having other college mates loving me even though they associated with me few seconds the time we met. My secret was that I would maintain a professional smart attitude and read positive things like motivational books and the Old Book-The bible. The charisma I had at the university caused me to triumph every time

Passionate presence can be felt even in companies like a powerful magnetic force.That is why when names of greatest names of the richest people are mentioned in leadership seminars, you even feel the greatness of the person and you will feel the charisma which is the passionate presence in that person. This is the secret of all charismatic leaders and transformational leaders. The way in which they carry themselves when they walk, you can feel the grace and a magnetic effect in your spirit.

Success is in us. Our human spirits is a gift which we ignore, but we were created uniquely in the image of God with a dominion nature. The authority to dominate or conquer our destinies is in our selves -just inside us.We should deeply feel it and it helps to project excellence to whosoever we make contact with. A positive self image projects an exuberance of light and confidence when we walk, speak or as we do our day to day work. It is the source of creative imagination and the greatest potential in us to excel to higher dimensions like an eagle.

Relax to discover yourself

Learnado Davici a great sculptor was a creative imaginator who advises us to have a little time of rest and relaxation. Do not be a workaholic, a drunkard of work! Rest because resting invigorates your brains. For when you come from that resting, you are charged with creativity and your judgement will be surer and clearer without mistakes. Your faculties will be sharper and focused. If you remain working consistently without rest, your passionate presence diminishes and you lose power as well as judgement and concentration. Deeply built in us as humans, is a desire to excel.

Workaholic in business is good at times, but there is need for you to reward yourself with leisure. Most entrepreneurs fail in this area and sometimes lack a social touch with families and other human beings.They continue to cut and do not want to put the axe down for sharpening; hence they end up chopping their own hands working. Work, but do not exhaust your imagination, have time to rest. Read and study, but take time to reflect. Escape your daily routine and go a distance away to assimilate new energy from nature. Invigorate your passionate presence with power and next time when you come for work in your venture, exploits are bound to happen.

Chapter 7: Persistent entrepreneurs

'Its fine to celebrate success but it is more important to heed the lessons failure" .Bill Gates

The power to hang on

Persistence is an essential factor in propelling your dreams and turning them into monetary equivalent. The majority of business people are ready to bury their ideas, concepts or business plans overboard and give up at the very sign of financial misfortunes. Some keep plans shelved for years and fear to put them into action. This is different to big entrepreneur like Henry Ford, Carnegie, Rockefeller, Bill Gates, Thomas Edison who and many others. They had guts to attain their goals against all odds fighting against them. Moreover, they had a carbon steel mindset to challenges. Take note that most of the challenges we see today, they are stepping stones to others.

Software of persistence

The building of a fortune generally demands the software of persistence. No fortune can be realised without sweat. From a slave to a palace means toiling hard, from poverty to wealthy and from rags to riches is the pattern of many entrepreneurs. Their experiences were bitter, but they stood resilient and they kept on fighting. The motto is keeping on keeping on; never remove hands on the plough. The purpose of accumulating riches requires a definiteness of purpose. According to Napoleon Hill, the writer of the book, Think and Grow Rich, he explains that the starting point of all achievement is desire. When that desire is strong, great results follow. The weaker the plans, the weaker the results .The momentum you exert in the goals is proportional to the end results achieved.

Failure

"I have not failed. I've just found 10,000 ways that won't work." This is Thomas Edison the man who made the electric bulb.Failure is a stepping stone to success .There is a need to challenge odds and stand pretty tall. Winston Churchill, a man known for bravery, courage and enduring faith purports that, "Success is not final, failure is not fatal: it is the courage to continue that counts." Life is like a boxing ring where each boxer has equal opportunities before the match, but what goes in the ring may be pathetic. You may be given a TKO (Technical Knockout), but you may challenge back in the second match and be the winner. It will never count whether you had been knocked the previous fight, but you are now the winner.

There is only one thing that makes a dream impossible to achieve: the fear of failure." You must make a decision that you are going to move on. It won't happen automatically. You will have to rise up and say, 'I don't care how hard this is, I don't care how disappointed I am, I'm not going to let this get the best of me. I'm moving on with my   life."

Keep moving on

Truman Capote puts it that, "Failure is the condiment that gives success its flavour."It is a chord of harmony to the music of success. When you strum the strings, the other strings may be of failure, but at the end you will produce a debut masterpiece music. Only those who dare to fail greatly can ever achieve greatly. Helen Keller, at the age of 19 months, became deaf and blind. But that didn't stop her. She was the first deaf and blind person to earn a Bachelor of Arts degree. She kept moving on despite her negative situation or the stigma associated with disabled people.

Have no fear of perfection - you'll never reach it.

Perfectionist will never be entrepreneurs. When the going gets tough, the perfectionist will quit or will be seen out of the market. Business is like a race where the enduring ones will continue jogging. Besides them, will be graves of fainting companies and a whole bunch of liquidating companies on their knees, the ones who were once best. The ones that will rise up will continue the race and may become winners at final winning line. So mistakes are common, but be careful because they may be fatal. Theodore Roosevelt voiced out that, "It is hard to fail, but it is worse never to have tried to succeed."

There is nothing we can do to insure against failure in business. We may have insurance, but failure can come up unexpected. Most people are afraid to fail and that's the reason why we are employed at companies not self employed. For years, we get the change of a salary, whereas the owner is earning a living through his brains and take home millions. The majority are afraid to jump offboard, they are afraid to get injured financially. Failure is a great lesson and even Bill Gates accredits the lessons of failure to be royal diadems which are precious to him. Without failure we will not develop the carbon steel backborne in decision making.

Risk taking

Risk takers are rare individuals in life. No pain no gain. We should sacrifice our time paying for the great price of success. There is something embedded in the definition of an entreprenuuer.An entrepreneur is a person who sets up a business or businesses, taking on financial risks in the hope of profit. In fact he is an "undertaker" .Quite strange! This is the game of true business people, they risk for a greater return in future.

Chapter 8: Greatest leader's secrets

The real entrepreneur

Commonly, an entrepreneur is thought to be someone who engages in starting and running a business, but to me, starting and running a business simply equates to being self-employed – and 99% of self-employed people are not real entrepreneurs. Most self-employed people are stuck. They are stuck in a cycle of trying to pay bills each month, or maybe they are making reasonable money but they are working too hard. They sometimes get stuck in their inability to grow their businesses, or they can't get out of their comfort zone ruts that have become bad habits they don't know how to break. For the most part, entrepreneurs are stuck working far too hard and not getting fairly rewarded for it. Then who is an entrepreneur? Let us see first one of their unique steel character

Entrepreneurial drive

I believe that most people start a business in order to live a better and more fulfilling quality of life. However, due to negative personal programming, unfavourable circumstances, lack of education or inspiration, or the understanding that all good things take time and constructive progressive effort, most people become despondent and completely lose sight of their original intention in wanting to become an entrepreneur in the first place. The real entrepreneur on the other hand, lives a fulfilled, exciting life that is truly rewarding, both financially and spiritually. The real entrepreneur generates effortless wealth and has masses of free time to do truly meaningful things outside of his or her business.

Characteristics of the real entrepreneur

The Real entrepreneur owns a business that generates healthy profits and pays out wonderful dividends each year. They do not have to work in the business, but if they choose to, they only need to work a few hours a day or a few days a week. The REAL Entrepreneur is always able to see what is happening in the business from a distance and is able to go on long holidays at least twice a year without worrying for a minute whether the business is operating optimally. They are also able to spend more time with family and friends and dedicate however much time they want to helping your community in a way that brings them joy and great personal fulfilment. If you are not living the above or progressively moving towards it, then you are not realising your potential as a REAL Entrepreneur, but rather, you're staying a stuck and struggling entrepreneur. Hard to face? Yes, undoubtedly if it applies to you, but accepting *what is* is the only way to identify what is *not* working for you, and introduce positive new strategies to shift from a struggle to growing from strength to strength as you gain a firm footing in the direction of success.

Corley, who spent five years monitoring and analyzing the daily activities and habits of people both wealthy and living in poverty (233 wealthy and 128 poor, specifically), isolated what he calls "rich habits" — and many of them are simply patterns of thought "I found in my research that wealthy people are by and large optimists," he says. "They practice gratitude and look at happiness like a habit."

Rich habits research

Corley, who presents and explains many of his findings in his book "Rich Habits: The Daily Success Habits Of Wealthy Individuals" and on his website, defines "rich people" as those with an annual income of $160,000 or more and a liquid net worth of $3.2 million or more, and "poor people" as those with an annual income of $35,000 or less and a liquid net worth of $5,000 or less.

Here are 10 ways Corley found that rich people think differently, based on statements with which they identify.

1. Rich people believe their habits have a major impact on their lives.

"Daily habits are critical to financial success in life."

Rich people who agree: 52%

Poor people who agree: 3%

Wealthy people think that bad habits create detrimental luck and that good habits create "opportunity luck," meaning they create the opportunities for people to make their own luck. "When I looked at luck," Corley remembers, "a lot of rich people said they were lucky and a lot of poor people said they were unlucky."

2. Rich people believe in the American dream.

"The American dream is no longer possible."

Rich people who agree: 2%

Poor people who agree: 87%

"The American Dream is the idea of unlimited potential, that you can make it on your own," says Corley. In his study, the vast majority of rich people believed that wealth is a big part of the American dream (94%), and that the dream is still possible.

3. Rich people value relationships for professional and personal growth.

"Relationships are critical to financial success."

Rich people who agree: 88%

Poor people who agree: 17%

Not only do rich people feel that their relationships are critical to their success, but they put a lot of effort into maintaining them, making a habit of calling up contacts to congratulate them on life events, wish them a happy birthday, or reaching out just to say hello. "When I applied the hello calls and the life event calls to my own life," recalls Corley, "I ended up making another $60,000 as a result."

4. Rich people love meeting new people.

"I love meeting new people."

Rich people who agree: 68%

Poor people who agree: 11%

Hand in hand with valuing relationships comes making new ones. Rich people both love meeting new people and believe that being liked is important to financial success (in fact, it's a whopping 95% that believe in the power of likability, compared to 9% of poor people).

5. Rich people think that saving is hugely important.

"Saving money is critical to financial success."

Rich people who agree: 88%

Poor people who agree: 52%

"Being wealthy is not just making a lot of money," explains Corley. "It's saving a lot, and accumulating wealth. Many of the people I studied aren't wealthy because they made a lot, but because they saved a lot." He's trying to instil what he calls the 80/20 rule in his own children: Save 20% of your income while living on 80%.

6. Rich people feel that they determine their path in life.

"I believe in fate."

Rich people who agree: 10%

Poor people who agree: 90%

Poor people are significantly more likely to believe that genetics are important to becoming wealthy, and significantly less likely to believe that they're the cause of their own financial status in life. "Most of the wealthy people I talked to were businesspeople who weren't always wealthy," Corley explains, "but they had this attitude that they could do anything."

7. Rich people value creativity over intelligence.

"Creativity is critical to financial success."

Rich people who agree: 75%

Poor people who agree: 11%

While rich people are more likely to believe that creativity influences success, poor people are more likely to think that being "intellectually gifted" is critical. They're also more likely to believe that wealth is usually accidental. "If you look at my stats, you'll find that a lot of wealthy people were C students," says Corley. "There's more to wealth than just being smart."Just observe entrepreneurs like Bill Gates

8. Rich people enjoy their jobs.

"I like (or liked) what I do for a living."

Rich people who agree: 85%

Poor people who agree: 2%

"Many of the wealthy in my study loved their job — it's not an accident," says Corley. In fact, 86% of the wealthy worked an average of 50 hours or more per week (compared to 43% of the poor), and 81% say they do more than their job requires (versus 17%). Corley says it's related to the idea of creativity being important to financial success: "These people found a creative pursuit that could turn into monetary value. When you engage in a creative pursuit that can make money, the reward is often obscene."

9. Good health is critical to financial success."

Rich people who agree: 85%

Poor people who agree: 13%

"One of the individuals in my study told me 'I can't make money in a hospital bed,'" Corley remembers. "Wealthy people think that being healthy means fewer sick days, which translates into more productivity and more money."

10. Rich people are willing to take risks.

"I've taken a risk in search of wealth."

Rich people who agree: 63%

Poor people who agree: 6%

"A lot of the wealthy people in the study were business owners who started their own businesses," Corley explains. "They became successful because they were master self-educators who learned from the school of hard knocks." In fact, 27% of the wealthy people in Corley's study admits that they've failed at least once in life or in business, compared with 2% of the poor. "Failure is like scar tissue on the brain," Corley says. "The lessons last forever."

Chapter 9: Marketing

"I believe that if you show people the problems and you show them the solutions, they will be moved to act."Bill Gates

Marketing and creativity

Theodore Levitt, in his book called Marketing Imagination, one of the earliest marketers advocated that nothing in the business can be achieved without high spirits. It means the vision, mission, objectives should be full of life of the dream of the organisation. Marketing is a strategic part of the organisation helping in the crafting of sound strategies. The needs in the markets should be converted into monetary value and capitalised before many new entrants enter to share the cake. The managers or entrepreneurs should always have a strategic plan of the future development, but it must be customer centric or customer driven.

Importance of formal education

There is a debate among entrepreneurship literature as to whether they are born or made.Offcourse, most people are born business people, but it takes education to perfect that talent inside them. Education stimulates the faculties and helps the mind to focus well and helps in the analysis of information necessary for decision making. However, there are those born in the blood of money, but research shows that they never succeed if they neglect education. Some wise entrepreneurs without formal education have employed the educated staff as a security to their wealth and have realised that education is important to perfect knowledge into wisdom. Fewer for sure are those who come from the street and become rich. This is a strategy used by Alicko Dangote, richest man in Africa, a Nigerian billionaire .He created the Dangote Group through the assistance of PhD doctors who are well qualified than him. They are the think tanks to his group of companies.

Market research

Fewer business people engage in market research so as to find out marketing trends, needs of customers and the action of competitors. They just believe customers are happy in their segment and have the mentality that as long they continue to buy their products, it means that they love them, but soon forget that research is the key cornerstone to find out what exactly is happening. It does not mean a formal expensive research, but an informal investigation and a close study of the products of the competitors which can be a very wiser exercise.

Do not ignore competitors, because your business is moving now, for tomorrow you will be out of the business game play. This is important especially to those who market the service. There is a need to study aspects such as customer care, service delivery, uniqueness of service, quality of service, customer satisfaction, customer feedback and price of the service. Also benchmark against the leaders in the industries and concentrate on your key competences. However, some entrepreneurs like Apple have entered the market casting a deaf ear in the phone and smart phone industries and are now the leaders. Research may discourage you, so sometimes it is luck that some products lead in the market.

Coaching

Bill Gates quoted that, "Everyone needs a coach. It does not matter whether you are in basketball, a tennis player, a gymnastic or bridge player."It shows that greatest innovators have reflection of those ideas from experts who have the experience. In business, motivational speakers can be good coaches, but a coach should be someone whom you invest your confidence in. It could be your friend or a consultant. Expert advice saves company costs in the long-term. Iron sharpens iron, so make sure that in business you play with people stronger than you. Hope you get it right! Some advice is more than money; it is a gem which needs to be cherished. Coaching is critical especially when the entrepreneur is faced with a multi-million dollar decision. Hiring a consultant can save billions of dollars in evaluating the decision on board.

Competitive advantage

Like what I alluded before, benchmark against the best in the industry .Compare yourself with the best, but do not get discouraged if you can't reach their heights. You can stand on the shoulders of the Giants anyway.Queit innovative isn't so? You may serve the markets which are giants are ignoring; a market strategy called market niching.It involves concentrating your efforts to a small sizeable segment which big companies are leaving. The market segment should react to your marketing efforts and many companies have become giants by growing with that niche and finally ending up serving the majority of the market share

Network

Strategies to network your businesses are many. Take advantage of technology by opening a website which is visible at the click of the mouse to your clients. You may connect to LinkedIn, facebook, twitter and be visible on almost every social network. Create a savvy website and also create blogs where customers can like your products or suggest opinions about your company or products. Do not ignore these comments, they are a reflection of reality, so try to analyse them. Also make professional business cards, send free vouchers, free diaries and calendars to your distributors, attend workshops and seminars .Attend their ceremonies when invited or even joining a social club such as golf club for dragging big fish customers. Know where to get your customers .If you are a clever fisherman, you will fish in a river not in a mountain with birds. That sounds logical. Invest in these activities constantly even if you do not see the results now. This is wise because most entrepreneurs when they advertise, they want to see results now. Understand that maybe your adverts were actually re-assuring your customers that you exist or building a positive image about your corporate identity.

Chapter 10: Financial intelligence

"Live out your imagination, not your history" Steve Covey

Budgets

The most important rule in wealth creation is saving. Saving is a key secret which most rich or successful entrepreneurs have mastered. They save every dollar and do not use money as if there is no tomorrow. Always have a budget in your business and that is why business plan is essential .It measures how you will use the money in the future and also reports if you have overspend in certain projected costs. As simple as a budget is, most entrepreneurs operate without one and at the end of the month there is always an application of an overdraft with the banker. It is always good to have someone managing your money, for example your wife or a Personal banker. Have a saving plan at your company like:

- Monitor the telephone bill because employees may kill you
- Cut costs as possible as you can
- Replenish old stock first before new stock to avoid stock expiring or rotting
- Allocate certain standard costs per each cost centre   and have a variance analysis

why the costs are above the standard costs

- Have a petty cash voucher signed and recorded to account for small cash transactions .As small they may, they sum up to huge amounts.

Bookkeeping and accounting

Make sure you do not underrate the recording of financial transactions in your business. Be it a small, medium or a backyard office business, account for every cent. If you can't find a cheap consultant to do your books and you have someone good in accounting then give him the books. Remember, one day you may need a loan or an overdraft from the bank and you need to pay tax. The earlier the better, not a last minute rush. Some consultants require that you print out your bank statement so that they can load it manually in their Pastel or other sytems.Make sure you do that periodically and pay them.

My experience as a consultant in auditing has made me to realise that most business owners do use the credit card carelessly and the spending patterns are bad. Believe me, for instances, the moment a huge lump sum deposit gets in the account you will see that in the next following days there are several expenditures, sometimes five to six times swiping of the credit card for personal expenses. The deficit that will happen at the month end is unbelievable. The bank statement will be having an overdraft.You may think that they never made sales and they will be unpaid overheads which are always there.This leads to a debt spiral and poor cash flow management. I will discuss later about the debt trap soon.

Another key thing that most entrepreneurs forget is to get a financial report of the performance of the business. Rarely, most of the owners analyse the financial statements. Figures never lie and they clearly report your spending or saving behaviour. Make sure you have time to analyse them because you may find many things like overspending on expenses like bank charges, telephone bill and escalating fixed overheads. Sometimes you may find shocking news, for example fraud. By studying figures you can be detect pilferage, shoplifting or fraudulent activities by workers.

Long term Investments

Unlike the idea of squandering every fortune, think of some ways to save your money for the future development of your business. Buy unit trusts or shares, but first get advice from a reliable stockbroker. You may open a 32 Day account for savings put aside or find lucrative medium to long-term investments where you can lock your earnings. Always make sure you award yourself a salary so that you do not misuse the company money. There must be a current company account and a personal account and do not mix the two because accountants or consultants may have problems in classifying drawings, cash or classifying other business expenses.

Avoid spending cash for promotions which are misleading or venturing into businesses that promise a faster return without proper considerations. Have a meeting with your management or a consultant to get their views. Always have investments in businesses that are low risk in nature .If it's a risk taking venture, it must be a carefully calculated risk.

Debt trap

Debt is a trap that caused most business to wind up their operations and sink into the grave of failure. Debt is not a wise way of financing a business, but the best is personal financial savings .Avoid financing organisations that promise no collateral, high interests rates or any benefits such as an overdraft as incentives for your demise. The cash flow of the business must be managed and savings are the best type of sources of finance because they have no interest rates attached.However, they are circumstances where you can approach your bank for credit. Make sure it is a calculated risk because you may pay more than you earn in the future.Avoid moving with the business credit card for miscellaneous expenses, but use the personal card instead. Learn to self discipline yourself and draw a line between yourself and the Business. These two are different even if it's your business. The business is a separate legal persona or entity and you are the owner not combined. It must stand on its own. Even if you the owner inject capital from your savings, please take your capital back because it is a loan to the business otherwise the temptation of drawings can happen because your money is in the business.

To grow or remain small

This is a dilemma with most entrepreneurs. Some want to remain in the small category because they know that a big organisation demands in management and control. Remaining small may be good for flexibility and for niching purposes. Like what was discussed before, niching is whereby a business focuses to a smaller segment that response to a marketing effort. For example, an auditing consultants firm can remain small so that it can get the unserved clients of big accounting firms.

On the other end of the spectrum, it is a myopic idea to remain small because many small businesses are also entering the market and it may be a dog eat dog competitive situation. It's rather to benchmark against the best and grow like them, but having your key competences on heart. Some prefer a differentiation strategy whereby they offer services different from big Guys. Time and opportunities sometimes tell you whether to grow bigger or remain small.

Some entrepreneurs entered the lion's game to get a big share, compete with big competitors only to realise some barriers to entry very difficult to penetrate. The barriers were put by big players of the industry. Why can't you remain a small like a hyena or a wolf, but your business at the end is manageable, flexible and has less overhead costs. Hyenas and wolves wait for the remains left by the lion and in this case this strategy can work. At the end you are going to have your share without much effort.

Hope you gained an insight into the entrepreneurship imagination. The ball is in your hands to start roll your dreams into play, pause or start planning your business ideas.Remember,imagination is a gift ,but can be learnt by anyone. The sooner the better you put your plans into motion

###

Thank you for reading my book. If you have enjoyed it, won't leave me a review at your favourite retailer?

Thanks

Liberty Chidziwa

About the Author:

Liberty Chidziwa is business analyst, consultant in accounting, payroll and a marketing research consultant. He holds an Honours degree in marketing and business Studies. Currently, he is studying towards an MBA in project management to master his entrepreneurial flair. He is running Capricorn Consultants Pty in South Africa, a branch of Ree and Lee Accounting Business Consultants which was operating in Ondangwa Namibia. He is also the owner of Grantsock Investments in 100% ownership which is a secretarial accounting registration company. The author has a passion for entrepreneurial vision and helps much in small start up advice.

Expert more books to come soon in the following topics

Title 1: Business Plans for entrepreneurs
Title 2: Branded for greatness
Title 3: Research proposal secrets
Title 4: Mafia marketing

Connect with me on LinkedIn, Twitter and Facebook
Email address:libchid@gmail.com
Whatsapp +27730906169

www.ingramcontent.com/pod-product-compliance
Lightning Source LLC
Chambersburg PA
CBHW051301170526
45165CB00004B/1811